ep   et's

m the

r

INE
RD
N

AND

THE TARRANT GUNVILLE 'VAMPIRE' LAID TO REST

All this and more in an armchair guide to Dorset's past and your future

BY THE SAME AUTHOR

**A SERIES OF GUIDED WALKS BOOKS, WITH INTRICATE
MAPS AND EXCITING NARRATIVE, TO THE LESS
FREQUENTED PARTS OF DORSET**

THE NEW STOUR VALLEY PATH	ISBN 0 9519376 7 7
THE CRANBORNE CHASE PATH	ISBN 0 9519376 2 6
THE BLACKMORE VALE PATH	ISBN 0 9519376 3 4
CIRCULAR DORSET RAMBLES	ISBN 0 9530338 4 8
RAMBLES FROM DORSET TOWNS	ISBN 0 9519376 5 0
HILL WALKING IN DORSET	ISBN 0 9530338 0 5
MORE CIRCULAR DORSET WALKS	ISBN 0 9530338 3 X

Front cover picture is St Peter's Church, Portesham. See Page 32
Back cover picture is St Mary's Church, Tarrant Gunville. See Page 14

ISBN 0 9530338 2 1

Published by Green Fields Books
13 Dalewood Avenue. Bear Cross
Bournemouth. BH11 9NR

DEAD INTERESTING DORSET

CONTENTS

DEAD INTERESTING DORSET

INTRODUCTION

Dorset is blessed with the most delightful churches and, in the quiet acres inside their boundary walls, there are hidden short histories, instructions on how to live a rewarding life, and uplifting (and frequently humorous) inscriptions that tell us about some wonderful Dorset characters - great and small.

For centuries, tombs, graves and family vaults have been adorned with ornate or quite simple messages of appreciation for the lives of those departed and, in many instances, these have included the creeds by which local dignitaries lived their lives (quite often imbuing the deceased with a saintly glow).   Others, for example, show an extravagant appreciation of the value placed upon a wife and mother by a husband left behind.

And that's another thing.   There are many ways of depicting the departure of ones relatives for pastures new and, for your greater learning, I list here a few which I have found in Dorset:

...he was suddenly removed....

...put off his tabernacle of clay.

...changed this life for a better...

....passed from time to eternity...

...departed this life...

...departed hence to rest...

and - simply, but most infrequently:

...died...

This book is intended as a celebration of the diverse memorials to the beautiful people of Dorset.   Many of the inscriptions to be found in the nation's churches are just like the next one, but none the less sincere for that.   However, the ones which I have chosen are from all over the wonderful county of Dorset and are far from being 'usual'. Even if they don't all have a tale to tell, each is a unique example of the noble art of monumental composition and poetry in church furniture carving and ornamentation.

Much of the research for this book has involved many hours scanning the Reverend John Hutchins' thorough history of Dorset but, since he died in 1773, other contributors have added to his original work. About the time of the third revision, the Victorians came onto the scene and, strangely when considering their love of revised Gothic architecture, set about removing 'ostentation' from the walls of our churches. As a result, some of the best inscriptions have either disappeared completely or have been removed to less visible areas. For example, a memorial in Wimborne Minster to Isaac Gulliver Junr., son of Dorset's famous smuggler, was moved from a choir arch and positioned so high up the West tower that you need binoculars to read it.

Further researches at the Dorset Records Office uncovered many strange tales but, conversely, put paid to others which had proliferated throughout Dorset for many, many years. Some of the strangest are included in the chapter "Where are they now?" but I have avoided the more common tales, such as whether Thomas Hardy's heart is really buried in Stinsford church, or is it the cat who reputedly ate the heart before the ceremony. This story has circulated for years but there is no way of proving it one way or the other without a totally unacceptable exhumation.

I have, however, included the doubts about the final resting place of Isaac Gulliver, but only because it is part of a wider story.

Now, read on and I hope that you feel inspired to a little self-improvement - or just to a few chuckles when you read, for example, about the aged pipe-smokers or the creed by which all politicians should conduct their lives.

Most of all, just enjoy the charming and, at times, light-hearted inscriptions which are shown here. Sadly, some have been obliterated by time, but others are still to be found if you care to pay a visit.

DEAD INTERESTING DORSET

TOP: ST MICHAEL'S, STINSFORD.....PAGE 10

BOTTOM: ST MARY MAGDALEN, FIFEHEAD MAGDALEN.....PAGE 5

CHAPTER ONE - A WORD TO THE WISE

A FEW SALUTARY TALES.

Ever since people began emblazoning tombs and memorials with escutcheons, cherubs, scrolls and the written word, we have been able to glean much wisdom from their earnest words and, whilst some are dire, many are quite humourous.

St Mary Magdalen, Fifehead Magdalen

This is my own favourite - it's so brief and to the point.   A mural monument to the 18th Century Davidge family bears this inscription:

> Stop passenger, and cast an eye,
> If thou art old, prepare to die;
> If thou art young, prepared be,
> Death may this moment seize on thee.

- and there could be no better illustration of the point that this inscription seeks to make than this next one -

St Nicholas', Child Okeford

An inscription in the body of the church reads:

> **In memory of CHARLES COX, late carpenter's mate
> of His Majesty's ship "Crescent" who was
> unfortunately
> killed by a musket ball fired from the
> shore by Edward Nexton, surgeon's mate, of
> the "Sceptre" at the Cape of Good Hope, on
> the 18th July, 1796, aged 25 years.**

If Mr Nexton was trying to drum up some business, he seems to have gone a little too far.   It seems that guns have always had a propensity for ending up in the wrong hands - even two hundred years ago.

St Gregory's, Marnhull

On an altar tomb in the churchyard you will find the following exhortation:

> **Thou stander-by,**
> **First learn to live, and then to die.**
> **As thou art, so once was I.**
> **As I am so must you be;**
> **Therefore prepare to follow me.**

> **SAMUEL STEPHENS died April 16, 1739, aged 51**

Although the perils of smoking are well publicised, John Warren, the parish clerk, who died at the age of 81 on 23rd January 1698, and Ruth his equally fortunate wife, seem to have enjoyed the dreaded weed for many a year, as the following inscription on their churchyard tomb testifies:

> **Here under this stone**
> **lie Ruth and Old John,**
> **who smoked all his life,**
> **and so did his wife.**
> **And now there's no doubt**
> **but their pipes are both out.**
> **Be it said without joke,**
> **that life is but smoke;**
> **Thou you live to fourscore,**
> **'Tis a whiff, and no more.**

St John the Baptist, Bere Regis

Low on the north wall, there is an altar tomb made of freestone with a canopy supported by four pillars, under which is a portraiture of a man and a woman in gowns, kneeling in prayer.

Between them, brass plates carry this inscription in Old English characters (see the next page):

If each things end doe each things worth expresse,
What is manes life but vayne unperfectnes;
How swiftlie rune we to our fatall ende,
Which have no hope if death be not our friende;
I, Skerne, doe show that all our earthlie truste,
All earthlie fayers, and goods, & sweetes are dust.
Looke on the worldes insyde, and looke on me,
Here outsyde is but painted vanitie.

Erected and finished by Margaret Skerne, his wife,
which caused this worke to bee made ano D'ni 1596

St Mary's, Wareham

A brass plate suspended on the south wall of the chancel bears the following dedication and instructions:

Here lyeth buried the body of William Perkins, of Byeastwall, nere Wareham, gent, who dyed the XXth of August, in the yeare of our Lord God 1613.

Fine witt, fat wealth, faire face, and sturdy strength,
All these devoringe death consumes at length.
Intemerated vertue and good name
Stand fast as rock, nothing removes the same;
Therefore love firme things, loath the fleeting still,
This is the sense and subject of my will.

St Andrew's, Yetminster

In the churchyard, there is a tomb with this hopeful, or worrying, inscription - depending on your point of view:

Thomas Read, died 19 Feb, 1797, aged 77

How strangely fond of life poor mortals be,
How few who see our beds will change with we,
Yet, serious reader, tell us which is best;
The toilsome journey, or the travellers' rest.

For my own part, at least in this context, I must confess that I go along with the old adage that it's often better to travel hopefully than to arrive.

St Peter's, Purse Caundle

This inscription isn't on a tomb but its sentiments could be intended as a warning to all clock-watchers.   It appears on the face of the church clock:

> Johannes Biddlecombe fecit, anno Domini 1731
> Richard Cox, churchwarden

> I am not welcome to come here,
> By some who love the world so dear;
> Yet I will tell how time doth fly,
> Because in time we all must die.

St Mary's, West Stour

This poetic masterpiece is probably the best example of the uncompromising style anywhere - certainly in Dorset:

> Here lieth the body of MR. MARTIN MEATEYARD who died February 14, in the year of our Lord 1733, and in the 63rd year of his age.

> BEHOLD ALL YOU THAT HERE PASS BY
> THIS HOUSE OF CLAY WHEREIN I LY;
> YOUR MORTAL STATE BEHOLD AND SEE,
> FOR AS I AM SO MUST YOU BE.

All very well, but perhaps it's time to we all moved on to the next chapter - where everything isn't doom and gloom.

CHAPTER TWO - INSPIRATIONS

LITERARY GIANTS IN DORSET

Dorset's literary contribution to the world is usually considered to be the works of the legendary Thomas Hardy and William Barnes, but it has been home to many more world-famous authors and poets - some for several years and some just passing through.

Bovington was home to T E Lawrence whilst such luminaries as William Wordsworth and Charles Dickens also stayed awhile in Dorset. Wordsworth and his sister Dorothy lived at Racedown Lodge, near Bettiscombe, between 1795 and 1797 whilst Dickens stayed for some time next door to the Tivoli Theatre in Wimborne. (Oh, alright. It wasn't the Tivoli then). Virginia Woolf holidayed in Studland in 1910 and 1911, and even Beatrix Potter and Enid Blyton enjoyed childhood holidays in Dorset.

I don't intend to give a history of these revered names, but I would like to pinpoint a few ecclesiastical monuments in Dorset which provided inspiration to both the great resident author Thomas Hardy and the visiting Charles Dickens.

St Cuthburga's, Wimborne Minster

On his many visits to the Minster, living less than 1/4 mile away in West Borough, Dickens could not have failed to see the following monumental inscriptions:

In memory of ELIZABETH SNODGRASS, who died at Wimborne the 9th day of November 1836, aged 64 Her mortal remains are laid in the ground on the West end of the Minster.

In a vault near this place are deposited the remains of JOHN BAYLES WARDELL of Arne, in the county of Dorset, who departed this life April 15, 1810, aged 8 years

As 'Pickwick Papers' has reached the four corners of the Earth, Mr Snodgrass and Mrs Bardell (he only changed one letter) have been immortalised far beyond the confines of Wimborne Minster.

St Michael's, Stinsford

In the North aisle, there is a 'very neat monument of white
marble, adorned with a pediment, columns, urns and cherubim.
Under the escutcheon there is a crest' bearing this inscription:

**Near this place are interred
AUDLEY GREY, esq and MARGARET his wife.
He was second son of Angel Grey,
of Kingston Marleward and Bridport
in this county, esq.
etc.
etc.
etc.
They had issue, George, Henry and Audeley,
who all died unmarried.
LORA,
their only daughter and heiress, who
married George Pitt of Stratfield Say, in Hampshire, esq.
(By whom she had four sons and five daughters),
erected this monument in pious memory
of her most honoured parents,
An. Dom. 1723**

*(By virtue of Lora and George's offspring, they almost rate a
mention in the 'Multiplication Table' of Chapter 3 - but not quite.
And, yes, this is the George Pitt whose monument would make an
inspirational politicians' creed - in 'Miscellaneous').*

However, Thomas Hardy would have been very familiar with this
monument, having sat close to it over many years through no end
of interminable sermons.   It has even been suggested that he
actually knew the inscription by heart.   Anyway, consciously or
not, Angel Clare became one of Hardy's enduring characters - in
'Tess of the D'Urbervilles' - and he can surely be traced back to
this church.

CHAPTER THREE - MULTIPLICATION TABLES

A LEAGUE TABLE OF OFFSPRING - IN ASCENDING ORDER

The fresh, clean Dorset air has proved beneficial to residents and visitors over the years. This isn't a recent phenomenon, although Bournemouth, the main attraction for recuperating gentlefolk in the Victorian and Edwardian eras, has only been in Dorset for the last three decades. Dorset has produced many large families in the past - and, apparently, it still does to this day.

THIRTEEN

All Saints, Manswood

The 1620 Uvedale monument, made from various types of coloured marble, shows the pedigree of the Uvedales of Manswood and More Crichel back to Henry Uvedale who died in 1518.

Near the aisle entrance, on a brass plate affixed to a gravestone, there is an effigy of a woman with her hands joined in prayer. The inscription includes such overwhelming praise that she must surely have been the most valued wife in Dorset (or was that Mary Ainslie in 'Modesty Forbids' - or Isabella Chudleigh in 'O.T.T.'?):

**Isabel Uvedale lieth here, that was the virtuous wief
of Henry Uvedale, esquier, and brought him by her lief
Thyrtene childerne to his joie, well nurtured by her daies
to live and lerne the redie waie to everlasting praise.
And of Anthony Erneley, esquier, of Wiltshire daughter she,
In whome there wanted no good gifte that in a wief shuld be,
For wisdome, manners, modestie, discression, love and curtesie,
With menie a conninge propertie to graft in her jentilitie.
Death cannot take awaie her praise, thoughe she be laied in grave,
But here in brasse her due desertes perpetuall fame shall have.**

She dyed ye xxiii of January in ye xvth yere of ye reigne of our sovereign ladye Elizabethe, Ao Dni 1572

FIFTEEN

St Michael's, Steeple

On the South wall of the chancel, there is a monumental slab of black marble set in a frame of alabaster. Upon it is the following inscription - just to prove that multiple procreations aren't necessarily weakening, (although the lady in this partnership did go to her rest at an age ten years younger than her husband):

In this chancel under a marble stone doe lye the bodies of FRANCIS CHALDECOT esq. and EDITH his wife, younger dautr and coheire of William Chaldecot of Quarrelston, in Dorset, esq. who were liberal constant housekeepers, bountiful relivers of the poore; carefull breeders of the children in piety and vertue; diligent and devout comers to the church, though it were very painfull unto them in their latter times, by meanes of age and other infirmity, 53 yeares and upwards they lovingly lived in chast wedlocke, and have issue 15 children, whereof 3 sons and 7 daughters came to mature age, and were most of them in the life times of their parents matched with ancient families of worship, most of them having fayre issues.

He died on Thursday ye 19th May, 1636, aged 85.
She on Thursday ye 23rd Augst, 1638, aged 75.

St Cuthburga's, Wimborne Minster

On a gravestone on the floor in the North aisle:

To the memory of ROBERT RUSSELL, of Kingston Lacy, gent, who died Jan 25, 1718; and ELIZABETH his wife, daughter of Nicholas Hookes, of Stockwell, in the county of Surrey, esq. who died Jan 3, 1735. They had issue fifteen sons and daughters, twelve of who are here interred.

Sadly, infant mortality was terribly high at that time.

NINETEEN

St John the Baptist, Bere Regis

Within the rails of the altar, there is a gravestone with this dedication:

Here lyeth the body of ROBERT WILLIAMS, second sonn of John Williams, of Herringston, knight, who deceased the 60th year of his age, Sept 5, an'o D'ni 1631; and of MARY, the wife of the sayed Robert Williams, daughter of John Argenton, gent, who deceased the 44th year of her age, Octob. 3, An'o D'ni 1630, who had isshew of thear bodys eight sonnes and eleven daughters.

AND THE WINNER IS - (Pause for loud applause) - - - WITH TWENTY CHILDREN:

Sts. Peter and Paul, Blandford Forum

Hutchins recalls the following ornate monument, and I quote - 'Between pillars of the south aisle of the chancel, a playne altar tombe of marble. On the top are pictures of a man in armor and a woman. Also a picture of sixteen sons and four daughters. Inlaid in brass on the West end':

Here lyethe buried Sir John Rogers of Braynston, Knight, Steward of this town of Blandford, who married Katrine, the daughter of Sir Richard Weston, Knight, and had by her sixteen sons and four daughters, which Sir John Rogers died the 22nd day of July, at Beket, in Berkshire, at the house of my lady Essex, and from thence brought to this towne of B. and buried under the T. 16 of Aug 1565

(Note: B = Blandford and T = tomb)

DEAD INTERESTING DORSET

TOP: ST MARY'S, TARRANT GUNVILLE (north side).....PAGE 15

BOTTOM: EASTBURY HOUSE ENTRANCE GATES.....PAGE 16

CHAPTER FOUR - WHERE ARE THEY NOW?

A FEW LITTLE LOCAL DIFFICULTIES

In searching out the unusual and most intriguing items of church and churchyard 'furniture', I have come across a few strange stories and, in attempting to find satisfactory explanations, have sometimes come up against a lack of written evidence in church registers (or anywhere else) which would either corroborate or invalidate the hitherto accepted versions of events.   Other tales have been, thankfully, clearly confirmed or utterly refuted.

PART 1: St Mary's, Tarrant Gunville - The Legend of the Vampire

Popular folklore has brought us the tale of William Doggett, supposed steward to Lord Melcombe at the nearby Eastbury House in the 18th Century.   Two books, which were published in the late 1980s, reproduce the tale as follows:

*William Doggett was Lord Melcombe's steward at the time the extravagant building was being erected and when the steward found himself in financial difficulties he appropriated some of the . building materials to raise funds for himself....*Peter Underwood: Ghosts of Dorset

*Dodington was created Baron Melcombe in 1761, the year before he died and enjoyed a national reputation for corruption, as did his steward locally....*Rodney Legg: Mysterious Dorset.

Hearing that his employer, Lord Melcombe, was returning to the house and being in imminent danger of exposure -

a) ...the wretched steward went into the library and shot himself - Underwood

b) ...Doggett did the first decent thing of his life.   He went into the library, closed the door, and shot himself - Legg, quoting the tale as told in the late Bugle Horn Inn.

William was supposedly buried, *'in the time-honoured manner for suicides',* on the unconsecrated north side of the church tower.   It is said that, during the 1843-5 Victorian rebuilding of St Mary's,

Doggett's grave was opened and the body re-interred.   The quoted legend claims that Doggett's body was

 a) ..*'fresh as the day it was buried and on the legs were tied yellow silk ribbons '* - Underwood

b) ..*'not decomposed and the legs were bound together with a ribbon of yellow silk'* - Legg

Both reports repeat the local belief that Doggett had become a vampire.

A continuation of this legend maintains that, *'at certain times, at midnight, his ghost waits at the main gates and catches a ghostly coach which is driven by a headless driver and pulled by headless horses.   The coach takes him up the drive to where the library once stood and Doggett descends from the coach, walks into the library and shoots himself.'*

Now, let's look at the facts which will completely exonerate William Doggett from any guilt in all of this.

1 .   Construction of the enormous Eastbury House, designed by Sir John Vanbrugh and costing £140,000 to complete, began in 1718 with the building of the utilities.   The house itself was started in 1724 and, although Vanbrugh died in 1726, building continued until it was finished in 1738, rivalling his other magnificent creations, Blenheim Palace and Castle Howard.

2 .   George Bubb, son of a Weymouth chemist and nephew of George Dodington had inherited the land and *'raised himself to the peerage under the title of Lord Melcombe'*.   He assumed his uncle's name of Dodington.   It was this George Dodington who built Eastbury House and, after a career in the service of Georges I to III in which *'he exhibited, amidst a heap of trivial details, a singular chain of gross venality and low intrigue, and demonstrated the influence of petty occurrences in the administration of public affairs'*...he became M.P. for Bridgwater, Weymouth and Melcombe Regis. He was created Baron of Melcombe Regis in 1761, the year before he died, childless, in 1762.

Consider these dates: The house was finished by 1738 and Dodington died in 1762.   Between these dates, William Doggett is supposed to have shot himself.

Now consider the history of the almost complete demolition of Eastbury House and the subsequent ownership of its remaining parts :

3.   After Dodington's death, all of the house furnishings were sold in 1763 and the house was demolished between 1779 and 1782.   The Society of Antiquaries have a watercolour dated c. 1780 showing the house in course of demolition.   This is reproduced in the relevant Royal Commission on Historic Monuments 'Dorset' volume.

4.   The house had passed by Dodington's will to his cousin Thomas Windham of Hammersmith.   He died in 1777, and his estates passed to Henry Penruddock Wyndham.   From him, Eastbury descended to Richard, 1st Earl Temple, who initiated the demolition.   He died in 1779, and the house passed to his nephew George Nugent Grenville, 2nd Earl Temple, aged 25 years, who was created Marquis of Buckingham on 30th November 1784.

5.   The only surviving parts of the original house are two parallel ranges, formerly stables, which stood on the North of Vanbrugh's forecourt.   These were left uninhabitable for many years, until being joined together into a fair-sized property in about 1800.   This new house was later rented by Thomas Wedgwood, son of the famous potter.   It was then purchased by James John Farquharson, whose descendants still owned the property in 1972.

But what has all this to do with William Doggett?

6.   If, as has been claimed, he was the steward who shot himself during the building of the house, the latest date on which he could have died would have been **1738** - See 1.

7.   If he had shot himself at any time during Dodington's life, he must have died, at the latest, by **1762** - See 2.

8.   William Doggett could not have been George Dodington's steward *'at the time the extravagant building was being erected'*. As we have seen, Dodington died in 1762 but research shows that William and his wife, Elizabeth, weren't even in Tarrant Gunville until, at the earliest, the winter of 1769/70.   Their second daughter, Elizabeth, was born in Blandford Forum, being baptised on 13th March 1765.   Anne was born before the family came to

Blandford. Now, before the girls came to Tarrant Gunville with their mother and father, the Doggetts third child, a little boy named Thomas, was also born in Blandford. He was baptised on 18th June 1766 but, sadly, before their final move to Tarrant Gunville, Thomas died, aged just three, and he was buried on 18th October 1769 at St Hubert's at Corfe Mullen.

So, seven years after Dodington died, the Doggetts hadn't even arrived in Tarrant Gunville.

So, now we know. William Doggett could not have committed suicide whilst employed as steward to either Dodington or Temple.

But, to cover the possibility that William Doggett really did commit 'suicide' over his rumoured stealing of building material, this must have happened during the demolition of Eastbury House, not '*at the time the extravagant building was being erected*', and William must have been employed in some other capacity.

In his 2002 book, 'Dorset Families', Rodney Legg repeated the tale, but changed Doggett's employer from Baron Melcombe to Lord Temple.

But, as we have seen, after Dodington's death, the property passed to Thomas Windham of Hammersmith, who died in 1777. Then, in rapid succession, via Henry Penruddock Wyndham, the house came to Richard, 1st Earl Temple. He died in 1779, aged 67, having been unable to find anybody to rent the extravagant property from him, and having initiated its demolition. His successor George, 2nd Earl Temple, finished the demolition which, as we have also seen, was completed by 1782 at the latest.

9. Therefore, if Doggett was employed by Earl Temple, in any position that would have enabled him to '*appropriate some of the building materials to raise funds for himself..*', then he must have committed suicide by **1782**. **But William died in 1786, four years later.** The entry in the St Mary's Parish Church, Tarrant Gunville Register for 1786 reads 'Buried. Mr William Doggett. June 23rd'.

One other remote possibility must now be expunged. What if William Doggett committed suicide for any other reason.

10. William's wife, Elizabeth, had died and been buried at St Mary's on 24th June 1785 - almost exactly a year before William. The parish register carries entries for both William Doggett's and Elizabeth's burials, whilst William's is the only entry on several pages to show the title 'Mr'. All others simply bore the Christian name. This confirms the respect of the Rector at the time towards Doggett and indicates that, if he was a 'suicide', at least his death was being treated as normal.

11. Their daughter, Elizabeth married Christopher Fleet, a minister and second son of Edward Fleet, the Rector of Tarrant Gunville, on 26th March 1794 . (Edward Fleet Junr., Elizabeth's brother-in-law, was the Rector who buried William). Her sister, Anne married Roger Claville, Rector of Manston on 17th September 1795. Anne and Roger went to live in the Rectory at Manston where they had two children, Caroline Anne and Elizabeth Jane, both of whom were baptised in 1803. Elizabeth and Christopher later moved to the Rectory at Lockerley, Near Romsey.

So, briefly, Elizabeth Doggett married a minister, later to be the Rector at St Mary's, whilst Anne married the Rector of Manston. If their father had been a 'suicide' these marriages would never have been allowed.

12. Much has been made of the fact that William Doggett's grave is not marked in the churchyard, and that he was buried in unconsecrated ground to the north of the tower because he was a 'suicide'. There is no evidence to support these ideas since:

Firstly, with an average of seven burials every year between 1786 and 1843 (when restoration started on St Mary's), 400 new graves should have been marked over that period alone - so where are they and why is nobody querying *their* whereabouts? - and:

Secondly, at St Mary's, most graves are situated on the north side because the church sits very close to the south boundary wall of the churchyard. So, most of the churchyard available for use as a burial ground lies to the north.

Now we know for sure that William Doggett was not only innocent of the charges of theft, but he didn't even commit suicide. So, what about the 'vampire' myth?

13.   As we have seen, on the previous page, the position of his grave is entirely irrelevant, and so are the 'yellow silk ribbons'. One story says that such ribbons were tied '*on his legs*' whilst the other says that his '*legs were bound together with a ribbon of silk*'.   Research into vampirism, essentially a European subject, has failed to discover a single word about ribbon of any colour.

14.   As for these items being a means of identifying William Doggett in an unmarked grave?   It was not the fashion in 1786 to wear ribbon on the bottom edges of the short knee britches - except amongst fops at court.   Medium or large square buckles were normal, even in the country.   If William Doggett had a penchant for such wear at the time, it is highly unlikely that there would have been anyone alive in 1845 who would have remembered such a minor affectation of sixty years before.   Then again, the second story says that his legs were '*bound together*' with ribbon.   So, how could he have left the grave without falling over?   Silly, I know, but no less fanciful than the whole 'legend'.

With the exposure of the false elements in this whole story, there can be no further grounds to maintain that William Doggett was anything other than a respected family man who had recently lost his wife, who had two daughters to support and who wanted to do just that - his death being mourned by his daughters, his friends and Tarrant Gunville villagers alike.

Postscript: Near the South porch on the outside flint wall of the chancel of St Mary's, there is a stone memorial to Sir Thomas Dacombe, who was the rector here in 1549 and who died in 1567, two hundred years before these events   The inscription confirms the concept of 'dust to dust' which, even without any research, renders the Doggett legend insupportable:

HERE LITHE S T D PARSON
ALL FOWRE BE BUT ONE
EARTH, FLESCHE, WORME AND BONE
M CCCC LX VII

Not all that comforting really, is it?   But then again, the legend of the **'Vampire of Tarrant Gunville'** is well and truly put to rest - and I hope William Doggett can rest as well, with his reputation fully restored.

PART 2: Canford Magna Parish Church - The Search for Nineveh

In the churchyard, there is a red marble altartomb inscribed:

THE RIGHT HONOURABLE
SIR HENRY AUSTEN LAYARD G C B,
THE DISCOVERER OF NINEVEH,
SOMETIME MEMBER OF PARLIAMENT
AND H M AMBASSADOR AT CONSTANTINOPLE.
BORN AT PARIS 5, MARCH 1817. DIED IN LONDON 5, JULY
1894.

Nothing really remarkable about that, especially as 'Nineveh Court' stands on the east end of the nearby Canford School (once Canford Manor - the home of Sir John Guest in the 19thC) and a stone over the entrance reads **"These sculptures were brought from Nineveh and presented to Sir John Guest, Bart., by Henry Layard in the year 1851"**. However, all is not as it seems.

Layard was subsidised by Stratford Canning, British ambassador to Turkey, to carry out excavations in Mesopotomia to find the elusive capital of the Assyrian empire - Nineveh. Having failed to find the city at the generally accepted site near the modern city of Mosul, Layard moved his operations twenty miles to the south. He found masses of artefacts and sent them to the British Museum. His book 'Nineveh and its Remains 1848-49' brought him recognition and an honorary doctorate from Oxford University. Sadly, later translations of cuneiform tablets unearthed at the original site proved that Mosul was right after all and that Layard's claims were erroneous and he'd been digging in the wrong place.

Now, back to Canford church where Mr. Layard's 'tomb' is equally misleading. He isn't buried here at all - His wife is. Layard himself, after a later (more successful) political career, died and was cremated and interred in Woking, Surrey in 1894.

PART 3: St Cuthburga, Wimborne Minster - The Smuggler's Tale

On the baptistry wall, there is a tombstone bearing the name of "ISAAC GULLIVER" together with a minute remnant of a date which reads "1c "- a segment of 1822. This was originally laid over his tomb in the centre aisle of the nave but it was removed during the "disastrous" restoration of 1855.

Gulliver's history is fascinating but it isn't the purpose of this book to provide complete biographies. There is more detailed information available and a full biography is now in process of publication locally. For now, just let me tell you that our Isaac Gulliver is the second generation of three Isaac Gullivers, born 5th September 1745 to Elizabeth and Isaac of Semington, Wiltshire. Our Isaac also married an Elizabeth and, whilst they were living at Long Crichel, they had three children - Ann, Isaac the third, and another Elizabeth.

Middle Isaac pursued a career as the most famous pirate in Dorset, and his exploits are manifold. But, after accepting a royal pardon, (apparently achieved because of the useful information which he brought back from his trips to France) he became an entrepreneur dealing in wines. The source of much of his wine was somewhat dubious but this appears to have been overlooked by the authorities and he lived his charmed life to the age of 77.

His son, Isaac the third, is commemorated on an ovoid plaque high up in the West tower, opposite the stone to Isaac Senior, but you will need binoculars to see it. On 8th October 1796, Isaac senior's daughter, Ann, married Edmund Wagg of Burton House, near Christchurch, and he was included on Isaac's plaque because, in his will, he asked to be buried with his good friend and brother-in-law. The inscription reads:

SACRED TO THE MEMORY OF ISAAC GULLIVER, OF
LONG CRICHEL IN THIS COUNTY,
WHO DIED NOV. 3. 1798, AGED 24 YEARS,
AND OF EDMUND WAGG OF BURTON
IN THE COUNTY OF HANTS, ESQ. WHO MARRIED
ANN, DAUGHTER OF THE ABOVE ISAAC GULLIVER
ESQ. WHO DIED THE 7TH OF MARCH 1799, AGED 24
YEARS.

It is purely coincidental that both young men, related by marriage, should die at the age of 24, but Isaac contracted a fatal illness from 'sleeping in a damp bed in Sherborne'.   After a serious family 'falling-out' in 1797, when Ann 'eloped' with brother Isaac and all of Wagg's plate and linen, they were re-united and Ann returned to her husband to live quite happily at Downton in Wiltshire.

Edmund died at home, just four months after Isaac, whilst sister Elizabeth lived until 1839.   Ann, the sole inheritor of Wagg's estates, married again - to a Doctor Crawford.   They left Dorset and moved to Winchester where they lived to the ages of 60 and 61 respectively.

Smuggler-cum-entrepreneur Isaac Gulliver senior died peacefully and was buried in Wimborne Minster on 20th September 1822 by Rev John Baskett Junior - although popular rumour in Wimborne has it that he wasn't buried in the vault at all but possibly in the churchyard.   Entry No. 525 in the Parish Register doesn't pinpoint the exact interment site.

Whilst on the subject of smuggling, not all Dorset smugglers had such a long life, as is witnessed by the following episode.

St Andrew's, Kinson - Bournemouth's oldest village

On the North side of the churchyard, there is a headstone of a smuggler killed in a violent battle with the Revenue Men, who suffered losses as well.   Gulliver had a house nearby, called Howe House, and St Andrew's was a renowned favourite hiding place for contraband.   There are still rope marks on the tower parapets where brandy barrels and chests were hauled up into the tower.

The inscription on the stone protests the relative values of a little tax evasion when weighed against a man's life:

**To the memory of ROBERT TROTMAN, late of Rowd in the county of Wilts, who was barbarously murdered on the shore near Poole, the 24th of March 1765.
A little tea, one leaf I did not steal,
for guiltless blood shed I to God appeal;
Put tea in one scale, human blood in t'other,
And think what 'tis to slay a harmless brother.**

CHAPTER FIVE - FOR KING AND COUNTRY

THIS IS A FAR, FAR BETTER THING I DO.....

Dorset sent its fair share of young men to the Napoleonic Wars and, side by side with the Spanish, many of the county's young men fought and died in the, ultimately, successful battle to rid Europe of yet another tyrant.   Many of these brave men are remembered in simple plaques scattered to the four corners of Dorset.   Just a few of them are included here.

St Mary's, Wareham

On the North wall of the chancel are these marble tablets:

**To MAJOR CHARLES LEFEBVRE, of the Royal
Engineers, who was killed at Fort Matagorda,
on the 22nd day of April, 1810, aged 35 years.
To CAPTAIN GEORGE LEFEBVRE, of the Royal Horse
Artillery, who died on the 22nd day of October, 1812,
aged 35 years,
That the bravery, skill and zeal with
which these men served their country
may not be entirely unrecorded, these
monuments are raised by their affectionate brother.**

**To WILLIAM CALCRAFT, esq. late Major
in the 7th Light Dragoons, who died at Santa
Martha, in Spain, on the 22nd day of
August, 1809, aged 35 years.**

**To ROBERT CARD, late in His Majesty's
Navy, and of this town.   Zealous and
brave in discharging his duty to his
King and Country, after constant
employment during the war from his earliest
years, he was appointed First Lieutenant
of the Redwing, stationed to promote the
abolition of the slave trade, and died of
malignant fever off Whidah, on the coast
of Guinea, the 16th March 1826, aged 32 years.**

British military adventures in Africa and India also robbed Dorset of many of its young men, although others survived their exploits and lived into stately old age.   British naval and military history, including Indian mutinies and African uprisings, is well represented in the following memorials, and it will be seen that several of Dorset's soldiers and sailors reached the highest of ranks in their chosen professions:

Holy Trinity, Dorchester

Tablets on internal walls of the church include these memorials to several military members of the same family, some who died in battle, and the last one whilst tending the sick and injured:

Sacred to the memory of JOSEPH FRITH, esq. formerly quartermaster in the Royal Horse Guards Blue, and for upwards of 24 years adjutant of the Queen's Own Regiment of Yeomanry Cavalry, who died June 30th, 1855, aged 61 years.   Also of the following sons...... of the above and Mary his wife. JOSEPH HENRY FRITH, a lieutenant in the Bengal Army, who died June 15th, 1853, aged 28 years. HENRY-WILLIAM FRITH, a deputy assistant commisionary general, who was killed in action at Malagaek, on the West coast of Africa, May 20, 1855, aged 28 years.   Erected by the widow and mother of the above.

Sacred to the memory of WILLIAM MITCHELL FRITH, assistant surgeon H.M. 54th Regiment, who died on the 7th March, 1856, whilst on service with his regiment at Gibraltar, aged 27 years.   This tablet erected by Colonel William Yorke Moore, and officers, non-commissioned officers, and privates of his regiment, as a mark of their esteem.

All Saints, Wyke Regis

Mural inscriptions in the church honour the following military and naval young men:

Sacred to the memory of Lieut. SIDNEY HENRY SWAFFIELD, H.M. 51st Kings Own Light Infantry (fourth son of Robert Hassall Swaffield, esq. of this parish). He died of fever at Kurrachee, East Indies, on the 8th of May, 1858, in his 21st year. The officers of his regiment have raised a monument over his remains in India to mark the spot where they are deposited....

Sacred to the memory of HENRY GEORGE PAYNE, first Lieutenant of H.M.S. Hecate, youngest son of the late Rear Admiral Charles F. Payne. He passed from time into eternity Dec. 2nd, 1857, on board H.M.S. Hecate, on the S.W. coast of Africa, aged 26 years.

The Virgin Mary, Swanage

Another soldier who served Dorset (and England) in battle, only to succumb to the terrible Indian conditions, is this young Swanage man - remembered on a plaque inside the church:

Captain FREDERICK COVENTRY, of her Majesty's 29th Regiment. The life of this most amiable and promising young officer was spared in the battle field of Sobraon, but he fell a victim to the climate of India and died at Kussowlie, in Upper India, on the 29th July, 1846, in the 26th year of his age. His remains lie deposited in the burial ground at Kussowlie.

The preceding gentlemen all died in the service of their country but the ex-naval Lieutenant, who we read about on the next page, managed to survive nineteen engagements against the French fleet under Hawke. However, his downfall came much nearer to home - in a duel resulting from a dispute with his neighbour about hunting game.

St Andrew's, Charmouth

On a tomb in the churchyard, there is this inscription:

**To the memory
of JAMES WARDEN esq,
who fell in a duel, the
28th of April, 1792,
in the 56th year of his age.
He was created Lieutenant in his Majesty's
Navy in the year 1760, in which capacity he
served his country with reputation and
success.**

He was in dispute with a neighbour and former friend, Mr Bond, on the subject of game and, in the ensuing duel, Warden fired first but his shot passed harmlessly through Bond's hat.   Bond then fired and his shot pierced Warden's heart.   At the inquest, the coroners' verdict of 'wilful murder' forced Bond to flee abroad for his life.

Underneath the inscription to Warden, is the following sad addition:

To the memory of ELIZABETH NEWELL WARDEN who, after lingering upwards of six years, at length put off her mortal part, wasted with pining sickness, to be clothed upon with immortality on the 11th day of June, 1798, in the 48th year of her age.

Pride of place in this Chapter really has to go to the gentleman on the next page, who seems to have been involved on most fields of battle from the Mysore mutiny of 1789, when he was only 17 years old, through Spain in the Napoleonic War to Waterloo in 1815, when he was still only 43.

St Mary's, Frampton

On a tablet in the nave, a proud inscription reads:

To the memory of Sir COLQUHOUN GRANT, K.C.B. and G.C.H. who departed this life on the 20th day of December, 1835, aged 63.

This brave and gallant officer at an early age entered the military service, in which he rose to the rank of Lieut.-General.   During the Mysore campaign of 1789, he greatly distinguished himself and was present at the taking of Seringapatan. He commanded the 72nd foot at the capture of the Cape of Good Hope, and the 15th Hussars during Sir John Moore's campaign in Spain.   He was wounded at the battle of Sahagun, and fought at the action of Morales and the battle of Vittoria.   On the ever-memorable field of Waterloo, where he commanded a brigade, he had no less than five horses killed under him.   He was honoured by the personal friendship of his sovereign and the esteem of his contemporaries, and he left a name recorded in the annals of his country

I can just imagine the panic in those poor horses eyes when they were told, 'Grant wants you'.   But what a fantastic record.

This chronological list places some of these events in context:

1774	Warren Hastings is 1st Governor-General of India
1789	Mysore campaign
1804	Bonaparte becomes Emperor
1805	Battle of Trafalgar
1808	Spain occupied by French. Peninsular War begins
1815	Battle of Waterloo
1848/9	2nd Sikh War; Punjab annexed by Britain
1852	Britain recognises Independence of Transvaal
1854/5	Crimea War
1857	Great Indian mutiny (Sepoy mutiny)

CHAPTER SIX - BELLRINGERS

HEALTH AND SAFETY AT WORK

St Peter's, Shaftesbury

On the south wall of the belfry, there is the following inscription to *'an honest bookseller, of whose integrity many stories long survived in the town'* - Hutchins:

> **Underneath lieth the remains of ROBERT WOOLRIDGE who departed this life April the 15th, 1777, aged 74 years.**

....followed by these instructions to the church bellringers - failure to comply being fined by quite a tidy sum, as you will find from the second entry in this section:

> **Of all the musick that is play'd or sung,**
> **There is none like bells if they are well rung;**
> **Then ring your bells well if you can.**
> **Silence is the best for every man.**
> **Then in your ringing make no demur,**
> **Pull off your hat, your belts, your spurr;**
> **And if your bell you overset,**
> **The ringer's fee you must expect.**

Clearly, keeping your hat on was disrespectful, your belt could get caught in the bell-rope and your spurs could damage the mats.   To 'overset' the bell is to cause it to swing past its highest safe, vertical point. This causes serious damage to the wooden frame and involves much heaving and straining to get it back again.

On the opposite, north, wall of the belfry, is verse two:

> **What musick is there that compar'd may be**
> **To well tun'd bells' enchanting melody;**
> **Breaking with their sweet sound the willing air,**
> **And in the list'ning ear the soul ensnare.**
> **When bells ring round, and in their order be,**
> **They do denote how neighbours should agre;**
> **But if they clam, the harsh sound spoils the sport,**
> **And 'tis like women keeping Dover Court.**

Yes, I have spelt 'agre' right and, no, I don't know what is wrong with 'women keeping Dover Court' or what or where Dover Court is. I'd be pleased to hear from anybody who *does* know.

Church of the Holy Rood, Shillingstone

This inscription on a board in the belfry confirms the risks that bellringers take by getting it wrong, by intemperate language, by fighting or by dressing incorrectly:

> **Praise the Lord with lowd symbols, if**
> **you curs or sware in the time of**
> **ringing you shall pay three pence.**
> **There is no musick play'd or sung**
> **is like good bells if well rung.**
> **Put off your hat, coat and spurs**
> **and see you make no brawls or**
> **if you chance to curs or sware liares**
> **Be sure you shall pay sixpence here,**
> **or if you chance to break a stay**
> **Eighteen pence you shall pay**
> **or if you ring with spurs or belt**
> **we will have sixpence or your pelt.**

1767

It seems to me that, if you were of a fighting, swearing, cursing temperament, you would have been well-advised to give bell-ringing a miss. After all, you stood to lose up to three weeks' wages if you broke a bell stay and one week's wages (or your skin) if you didn't remove your belt or spurs. Hard times indeed.

St Thomas Becket, Lydlinch

Painted on the belfry wall is the following rhyme:

RULES TO BE OBSERVED BY RINGERS

> **Put off your hats, your belts and spurs,**
> **And when you ring make no demurs.**
> **Sound out the bells well if you can**
> **(Silence is best for every man).**

**But if a bell you overthrow,
Sixpence unto the clerk you owe.
John Hopps and John Young
Churchwardens, 1746**

At least, the fines were standard - as was the only word which any of the writers could find to rhyme with 'spurs'.

The Lydlinch notice had to be included here since these Lydlinch bells were made famous throughout Dorset - and farther afield - by the wonderful Dorset dialect poet, William Barnes.

Just a few lines will show you what I mean.   They're beautiful:

> When vrozen grass, so white's a sheet,
> Did scrunchy sharp below our veet,
> An' water, that did sparkle red
> At zunzet, were a-vrozen dead;
> The ringers then did spend an hour
> A-ringen changes up in tow'r;
> Vor Lydlinch bells be good for sound,
> An' liked by all the naighbours round

PICTURE: THE VIRGIN MARY, SWANAGE.....PAGE 32

READ AND INWARDLY DIGEST

Throughout the county, simple inscriptions give reminders to mourners and passers-by to look to the future - and to prepare for its inevitable conclusion.

The Virgin Mary, Swanage

On a brass plate, on a flat stone, in the middle of a pew opposite the porch:

> **Suche as I was, so be you,**
> **and as I am, so shall you be,**
> **And of the soule of John Harve**
> **God have mercy.**
> **The whiche decessed the xvii day of March, ye yer of**
> **Or Lord MVCX.**

Loscombe church, Powerstock

In the old churchyard, Hutchins recalls the Dawe family tomb:

> **Here lieth the body of WILLIAM DAWE, who**
> **died the 11th of August, Ano 1690, aged 84 years.**
>
> **As you are now so once was I.**
> **Endued with riches and prosperity;**
> **As I am now so shall you be,**
> **Cloathed with ashes, as you may see.**

And just one more - or, perhaps, this should have been included in the 'Dreadful Doggerel' chapter:

St Peter's, Portesham

In the churchyard, under the south wall of the church, there is a tomb which has a canopy supported by pillars, inscribed:

> WILLIAM WEARE HE'S HEERE IN DUST,
> AS THOU AND I, AND ALL MEN MUST;
> ONCE PLUNDERED BY SABAEAN FORCE,
> SOME CALL'D IT WAR, BUT OTHERS WORSE.
> WITH CONFIDENCE HE PLEADS HIS CAUSE
> AND KING'S, TO BE ABOVE THOSE LAWS,
> SEPTEMBERES EYGHTH DAY DIED HEE,
> WHEN NEARE THE DATE OF 63:
> Anno Domini 1670

St Mary Magdalen, Fifehead Magdalen

Now, everybody knows the old saying about 'one swallow doth not a summer make.....etc'.   Well, whilst researching for 'The Stour Valley Path' book many years ago, I came across the village of Fifehead Magdalen. In the churchyard, under a large yew tree, I found this inscription on an altar tomb (The blank is where the slab is chipped);

> The corps of Tho. Newman, gent
> Is here interrD AprIL V., 1668
>
> WHILST TOWER REMAINE, OR SPRING MY YEW,
> HERE I SHALL LIE AS GREEN, YOUNG, NEW,
> ....RE NEWS TO US GOOD TIMES SHALL BRING,
> ONE SWALLOW DOTH NOT MAKE THE SPRING

So which was first.   Fifehead Magdalen's 'Spring Swallow' or the more famous 'Summer swallow'?

CHAPTER EIGHT - DREADFUL DOGGEREL

WORSE VERSE

I don't know what it is, but the opportunity to extol ones loved-ones finer points in verse has lead to some of the most appalling poetry and inappropriate puns.   I have come across several instances of this in Dorset and, whilst quoting just a few, I recognize that they were all reverently composed and sincerely meant at the time.

Melbury Sampford, Strangways' Church

In the small, private church which stands in the park next to Melbury House there is a small brass plaque in the fascia at the east end of the church.   It is dedicated to a steward of the Strangways of Melbury Sampford, who died in 1779:

GEORGE DERNSTHORPE, esq.
"His body here is underneath,
we hope his soul is higher"
In grateful remembrance......

The above eloquent thought was composed by Thomas Davis, a farrier at Chantery.   The Rev. Mr. Jenkins proposed the following, delightful lines to accompany it:

I Thomas Davis did these lines indite,
And on this plate of brass the same did write.
I too did fix it to the chancel wall.
Long may it hang there and God save us all.

St Martin's, Bryanston

On the south wall of the nave, on a brass plate, there is a portraiture of a woman kneeling at a desk.   Behind her are her three sons and three daughters in the same posture.   The inscription is on the next page (and I hope you're good at maths):

Syr Andrew Lutterel's child and Richard Roger's wyfe,
Here Lutterel lys in tomb, exil'd from mortal lyfe.
By mother's syde extract from Wyndham's worthy lyne,
Who at her wedlock day had lived years tenne and nyne.
Seven years no child she had, yet after daughters five,
Sonnes three, which three she left, and daughters three
alyve.
What tyme years twente twice and three she had outworne,
her corps, which was of yearth, to yearth again was borne.
Not so her godlie soule; hither bound is in reaste;
Of such a godlie dame we may pronounce her blest.
Who died the x day of March, Ao. 1566

Chapel of the Nativity of the Blessed Virgin Mary, Beaminster

A brass plate in Hillary's aisle, which adjoins the open north side of the chancel:

Here lieth the body of ANN the wife of HENRY HILLARY of Meerhay, who died the.....of February, anno Dom. 1653

**"Tis not because this woman's virtue dies,
That the brass tells us where Ann Hillary lies.
Her name's long lov'd, she is in this commended,
The poor cry out, their Hillary term is ended.**

But then, I don't suppose many Dorset folk at that time were aware that the quarterly sessions of the Law Courts' sittings had names.

Holy Trinity, Chilfrome

On a slab on the chancel floor, there is the following inscription:

If you enquire who lies within this frame,
One much more CLEMENT by his life than's name,
A painful pastor that with Christ did gather,
a lovinge husband and a tender father.
Here resteth the body of THOMAS CLEMENT, clerk,
who deceased the 18th of June Ano 1675

And here we have another 'painful pastor' - who also took great pains to serve his flock.

St Andrew's, Bloxworth

In the churchyard, near the tower, on the South side:

Here lyes that reverend orthodox divine,
Grave MR. WELSTEED, aged seventy-nine,
He was the painfvll pastor of this place
Fifty-Five yeares compleat, dvring which space
None jvstly covlde his conversation wovnd,
Or's doctrine taint, 'twas so sincere, so sovnd,
Thvs having his long thread of life well spvnne,
'Twas cutt, November's tenth, in fifty-one,
1651

St Nicholas, Edmondsham

A gravestone in the churchyard attached to Edmondsham House bears the following rustic rhyme:

Here lieth the body of PERKINS JOHN,
In 1676 my glass begun,
In 1745 my glass was run;
And since that time I am dead and gone.
Whoe'rs alive that knew the man,
His vertues chuse, his vices shun

Maybe, his virtues were well known, and he had no known vices.

St Nicholas, Silton

This charming little poem, sadly, is no longer visible on its churchyard stone:

Here lies a piece
of Christ, a star of dust,
A vein of gold, a china dish
that must
Be wed in Heaven when Christ shall feast
the just.
Being on that pious woman JOAN, ye wife of
Robert NATION, who departed this life the 28th
of November, 1689, in the 29th year of her age.

Now, to finish. This pun-filled ditty is the pinnacle of doggerel epitaph writing, and shows the heights to which we should aspire. This art really should be practised more widely today.

St Martin's, Lillington

On a flat gravestone at the entrance to the aisle (formerly belonging to the Cole family of a local estate):

> **Reader, you have within this grave,**
> **a COLE rak'd up in dust;**
> **His courteous fate saw it was late,**
> **And that to bed he must:**
> **So all was swept up to be kept,**
> **Alive until the day**
> **The trump should blow it up and show**
> **The Cole but sleeping lay.**
> **Then do not doubt, the COLE'S not out,**
> **Thou it in ashes lies;**
> **The little spark, now in the dark,**
> **Will like the Phoenix rise**

Absolutely wonderful - and I rest my case.

PICTURE: ST NICHOLAS', SILTON.....PAGE 36

CHAPTER NINE - MODESTY FORBIDS

PRAISE BEYOND THE CALL OF DUTY

It appears that, throughout the centuries, it is the ladies who earned the highest praise and, with a few dedications to husbands and fathers thrown in to attempt an even balance, here are some short 'essays' on the most unbelievably virtuous people who could ever have walked this, or any other, county

St Osmund's, Melbury Osmond

The south east body of the church is adorned with a neat marble monument, the inscription on which, says Hutchins, *'contains a character that no mortal was ever entitled to'   The prototype is to be found at the Abbey Church in Bath which Mr Ainslie sometimes attended during his occasional residences in that city, though it is said, he had the vanity to pass it off, amongst his Dorsetshire friends, as his own composition'.*   Both the appreciative Mr Ainslie and the angelic Mrs Ainslie were employed in the household of the Strangway-Horners of Melbury House.

> In memory of
> **MRS MARY AINSLIE,**
> interred in a vault below this;
> died December 24th, 1757, aged 63,
> a wife of more than 21 years
> to Mr William Ainslie,
> who never saw her once ruffled with anger,
> or heard her utter a peevish word;
> whether pained or injured, the same good woman,
> in whose mouth, as in whose character,
> was no contradiction.
> Resigned, gentle, courteous, affable,
> without passion, though not without sense,
> she took offence as little as she gave it;
> she never was, or made an enemy.
> To servants mild, to relations kind,
> to the poor a friend, to strangers hospitable;
> always careing how to please her husband,
> yet not less attentive to the one thing needful.
> How few will be able to equal
> what all should endeavour to imitate.

There you are, ladies.   This may be the era of political correctness but it's not too much to ask, is it?

However, to even things up a little, the next examples, although much more brief, should induce some serious aspirations amongst the gentlemen.

St Mary's, Wareham

In the south aisle, there is a lofty marble monument, enriched with carvings.   The inscription upon it reads:

Near this place lie the remains of
ANTHONY TREW, gent, late of this town
whose life was truly adorned with integrity,
temperance,
and a strict observance of every social and relative
duty.
He died the 20th of Sept. 1771, aged 80.
Martha, his only child, widow of
George Turner, late of Penleigh, in Wilts, esq.
erected this monument
as a testimony of her filial affection
and unfeigned regard
for his eminent virtues.

Sts Peter and Paul, Blandford Forum

At the upper end of the north aisle is a mural monument to a very talented poet whose simple virtue was much admired:

In memory of CHR. PITT, clerk, M.A., very eminent for his talents in poetry, and yet more for the universal candour of his mind, and the primitive simplicity of his manners. He lived innocent, and died beloved, Apr 13, 1748, aged 48

On a black marble slab near the north door can be seen this inscription:

This tablet is erected in memory of RICHARD PULTENEY M.D. F.R.S., who after 36 years residence in this town, died on the 13th of October 1801, aged 71. That modesty for which he was remarkable through life, forbad any vain eulogium on his tomb, but he will long be remembered with gratitude and affection, both as physician and as a friend, and with the truest reverence and sorrow by Elizabeth his afflicted widow, daughter of John and Elizabeth Galton, of Shapwick, Dorset.

Elizabeth died 28 Apr. 1820, aged 81, and was buried with her husband Richard in the churchyard at All Saints Church in nearby Langton Long.

Right, it's the ladies' turn again and it's difficult to imagine a better eulogy than this - again at Sts Peter and Paul, Blandford:

On a gravestone near the north door:

> **Near this place are deposited the remains of**
> **MARY, wife of George Marsh, clerk, A.M.**
> **She departed this life Jan 30, 1787, aged 43.**
> **Many and great were her virtues, but sincerity,**
> **that virtue which discriminates the genuineness**
> **of all the rest, and gives them their lustre,**
> **was most observable in every part of her conduct.**
> **Resurgat in pace**

Now, this chapter ends with just a few more examples for your general guidance. The tablet which heads the next page is probably one of the first inscriptions in stone to give fulsome praise to capitalist tendencies:

All Saints, Langton Long

This little church is just a mile from Blandford Forum.   A monumental tablet in the body of the church reads:

> In memory of James Farquharson, of London, merchant, a man of strict probity, unwearied diligence, and unbounded benificence.   By his extensive and correct knowledge of commerce he acquired an ample fortune; his judicious disposition of which has raised many to opulence, who join with his relict in lamenting the loss of the tender husband, the good father.

Anne Farquharson, who erected this monument, died Feb 4, 1837, aged 84 .

St Mary's, Wareham

For the last word, we return to St Mary's to read of the wife of a Wareham draper in Henry VIII's time.   Hutchins recorded this inscription on a 'brass plate, without the altar rails':

> Here lyeth the body of Ann Franke, the wyfe of Richard Franke, sumtyme draper in Warham; she decessed the xviii daye of Apryll, in ano 1583, being then of the eayge of 30 yeres.

> A matron sage, in maners mild, in modistie did excell,
> In Godliness, in governement shee ever guyded well;
> In wedlocke chast in faythfull hand shee yelded up her lyfe,
> Beloved, bewayled by man, by mayd, and wyfe.

CHAPTER TEN - A TRIFLE O.T.T.

NOBODY DID IT BETTER

There are just two entries in this chapter. I had considered including them in the 'Modesty Forbids' chapter but, after many readings of the sentiments aroused by, and the approbation heaped upon, these two 18thC personages (one male, one female), I felt that they far outshone all others and deserved their own chapter.

Sts Peter and Paul, Cattistock

On a black and white oval tablet against the north wall of the Chalmington, or north aisle:

To the memory of DIANA, the third surviving daughter of the late Colonel George and Isabella CHUDLEIGH who departed this life at Chalmington, on the 8th day of March, 1794, in the 63rd year of her age. Her piety was ardent but rational; her charity, benificence and generosity (almost unbounded) were without ostentation. Exact in the discharge of all personal and relative duties, she was rigid only to herself; candour and lenity guided her opinion and treatment of every one besides; for she was truly liberal. Delicacy of sentiment, politeness of manners, and chearfulness of disposition refined and endeared her conversation, whilst her general knowledge was sufficient to make it interesting. Her whole conduct was uniformly consistent, because in every instance she acted from principle. Reader, enquire and examine how she lived, and then "go and do thou likewise"

Now, the praise for the gentleman to whom the memorial on the next page was raised is more in what is NOT said rather than in what IS said.

St Nicholas, Abbotsbury

In the south aisle, a brass plate inlaid in the floor carries this inscription:

To
the memory
of
the Reverend
JAMES HARRIS, M.A.
who departed this life
on the fourth day of May
A.D.
M.DCC.LXXII
in the sixty-fifth year of his age,
after having been Vicar of this parish
two and thirty years.
Expect not, reader, to find
the merits of the deceased
represented on this tablet;
Go,
learn his character
from
his family, his parishioners, his acquaintance;
and
imitate in thy own life
the virtues
which shall appear to have been displayed
in his conduct.

These little rites, lamented shade, receive,
The last sad tribute which thy friends can give.

And thus is displayed as much praise as was lavished on Diana Chudleigh - with a far greater economy of engraving.

CHAPTER ELEVEN - LUCKY DIP

A MISCELLANEOUS SELECTION

St John the Baptist, Buckhorn Weston

A few years ago, in Long Crichel, I came across a modern gravestone on which the designation of 'music critic' was engraved.   This follows a long tradition of including the more unusual occupations in memorials.   Here, on a flat stone in the chancel is the following dedication:

> John Sampson, Rector, here doth rest in Christ,
> Divine, physician, <u>anagrammatist,</u>
> He was baptised May 12, 1626
> He died June 18, 1715, aged 90 years
> Buried June 22, 1715

Definitely one of the more unusual occupations for very rural Dorset.

GOOD AND FAITHFUL SERVANTS

1. St Mary's, Iwerne Stepleton

In the retired churchyard, Hutchins recorded a fragment of a single gravestone which, when perfect, bore the inscription:

> **Near this stone JACK WEBBER lies,**
> **Rich as Croesus, as Solomon wise,**
> **He was born a fool, and died the same,**
> **Happy for all who can live and die like him.**

'He was a harmless idiot employed in the service of Peter Beckford esq. who probably caused the stone to be set up': Hutchins.

Really, many so-called 'simple' people were employed by responsible gentry and farmers. Most were found to give excellent service, within the limits of their capabilities, and such acts of kindness by an employer were often repaid by years of hard work.

2. St Michael's, Over Compton

The following memorials are to faithful servants of the Godden family of local renown - who were clearly much appreciated.

On the east and west sides respectively of the porch on the south side of the church, black stone monuments bear these inscriptions:

Sacred to the memory of
ONESIPHORUS BICKNELL
who was buried at the entrance of this porch.
He died of a decline,
on the fourth day of June, 1805,
aged 36 years

In memory of HENRY DYTE and SUSANNAH his wife.
He died 18 Aug, 1810, aged 84 years.
READER! IF IN AN HUMBLE STATION, GO AND IMITATE
HIS CONDUCT, FOR EXCEED IT YOU CANNOT.

He was bailiff to the Godden family for more than 60 years.

A SQUARE DEALER

St Michael's Chapel, Long Bredy

At the east end of the south aisle, on the south side of the nave, there is a monumental tablet for the Williams family and on it is the following inscription:

*To the memory of WILLIAM WILLIAMS, esq. of
Castle Hill in this county, for many years M.P.
for Weymouth, and Provincial Grand Master
of the ancient Society of Free and accepted
Masons for the County of Dorset.
This monument is erected by the brethren
of the Province of Dorset as a token of their respect and
esteem for the able manner in which he presided over
their masonic labours for more than 25 years.*

THE POLITICIANS' CREED

St Michael's, Stinsford

Famous for being the church where Thomas Hardy played his fiddle in the church band, there is much that politicians of today could learn from the handsome cenotaph which is at the west end of the north aisle.   Built from various coloured marbles, with urns and a fine bust of George Pitt, the inscription reads:

Sacred to the memory
of GEORGE PITT, of Stratfield Say, in the county of
Southampton, esq
who died Feb. 28, 1734, in the 72 year of his age,
and lyes there interred with his ancestors.
He was adorned with many virtues, both public and private,
A true and disinterested love for his country
banished from his mind all party prejudices and selfish views.
He always preffered the publick good to royal favour,
and the liberty of acting by the dictates of his
conscience to the enticement of honours,
which he had the fortitude to refuse.
In private life, he shewed himself far from affecting
Admiration or Popularity,
yet was his appearance venerable, and his
conversation endearing,
which acquired him both.
His universal benevolence and exemplary charity
bore so just a proportion to his affection for his family,
that, while he was the refuge of the poor and distressed,
and supported an hospitality suitable to his estate,
he made ample provision for a numerous issue,
and rendered the figure of his relict not unworthy of
her ancestors,
whose ancient seat at Kingston in this parish he rebuilt,
Such was he while he lived,
and dying, left to his descendants a valuable example:
to perpetuate which, as well as to give a lasting
testimony of her just regard
to her most tender and most beloved husband,
Lora, the only daughter and heiress of Audeley Grey
of Kingston afaoresaid, esq. erected this monumentt

And I'm sure the engraver of this inscription was mightily relieved when he reached the end without making a mistake.

THE SMALLPOX PIONEER

St Nicholas, Worth Matravers

A headstone in the churchyard, to a true pioneer in the field of preventive medicine, reads:

> **Sacred to the memory of BENJAMIN JESTY of Downshay, who departed this life April 16th, 1816, aged 80 years. He was born at Yetminster in this county, and was an upright, honest man; particularly noted for having been the first person (known) that introduced the cow-pox by inoculation, and who from his strength of mind made the experiment from the cow on his wife and two sons in the year 1774.**

His lovely, long stone cottage at Upbury Farm still stands in Yetminster, next door to St Andrew's church. The blue plaque on the wall opposite says that Jesty was born in 1736, confirming that he would have been 80 when he died. Unfortunately, Hutchins misquoted the inscription at Worth Matraver's church as saying that he was 70 years old.

BENEFITS OF PHISICK

St Mary's, Cerne Abbas

The Cockeram family of Cerne Abbas clearly owe some debt to the relative who is recalled on the small oak tablet in the north aisle:

> *Here under lyeth ye body of WILLIAM COCKERAM, gent, a practitioner in phisick and chirurgery, who died the twenty first day of January 1679, aged 43 years and 9 months*

Whatever he discovered, his descendants certainly lived a lot longer than William did. Robert Cockeram, yeoman, died Dec 1802, aged 90, whilst Thomas Cockeram died 1804, aged 88 and Jenny, Thomas' wife, died March 1784, aged 79.

THE ADMIRABLE REVEREND JOHN HUTCHINS

St Mary's, Wareham

On the chapel's North wall, there is a white marble monument with this inscription to the much appreciated gentleman without whom this book would have been impossible to write:

This small tribute
of respect
for the memory of
The Rev. JOHN HUTCHINS, M.A.
many years Rector of Wareham and Swyre,
and Author of
'The History and Antiquities of Dorset'
who died 21st June 1773, aged 75,
was erected by his son-in-law
John Bellasis, esq,
Major in the Service of the East India Company,
1792

PICTURE: ST MARY'S, WAREHAM.....THIS PAGE

BIBLIOGRAPHY

History and Antiquities of the County of Dorset:
Rev John Hutchins
Inventory of Historical Monuments in the
County of Dorset: H.M.S.O. 1970

PICTURE: STS PETER AND PAUL, BLANDFORD FORUM....PAGE 13

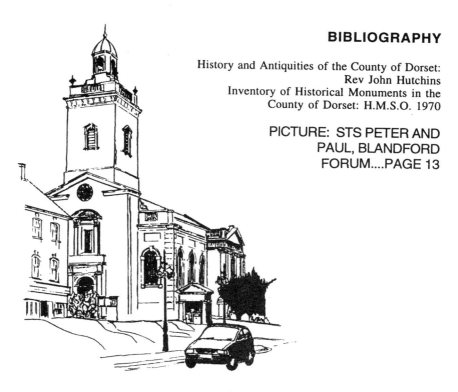

INDEX

49

INDEX

INDEX